GARBAGE COLLECTORS

Many thanks to the garbage collectors of North York
— P.B. and K.L.

Acknowledgments
Thank you to Joseph Giambra, Commissioner, Public Works, and
Maureen Skinner Weiner for taking the time to review the manuscript.

⚹ Kids Can Read ™ Kids Can Read is a trademark of Kids Can Press Ltd.

Kids Can Press acknowledges the financial support of the Government of Ontario,
through the Ontario Media Development Corporation's Ontario Book Initiative; the
Ontario Arts Council; the Canada Council for the Arts; and the Government of
Canada, through the BPIDP, for our publishing activity.

Published in Canada by
Kids Can Press Ltd.
29 Birch Avenue
Toronto, ON M4V 1E2

Published in the U.S. by
Kids Can Press Ltd.
2250 Military Road
Tonawanda, NY 14150

www.kidscanpress.com

Edited by David MacDonald
Designed by Kathleen Collett
Educational consultant: Maureen Skinner Weiner, United Synagogue Day School,
Willowdale, Ontario
U.S. reviewer: Joseph Giambra, Commissioner, Public Works, Buffalo, New York
Printed in China by WKT Company Limited

The hardcover edition of this book is smyth sewn casebound.
The paperback edition of this book is limp sewn with a drawn-on cover.

CM 04 0 9 8 7 6 5 4 3 2 1
CM PA 04 0 9 8 7 6 5 4 3 2 1

National Library of Canada Cataloguing in Publication Data

Bourgeois, Paulette
     Garbage collectors / written by Paulette Bourgeois ; illustrated by Kim LaFave.

(Kids Can read)
First published under title: Canadian garbage collectors.

ISBN 1-55337-573-4 (bound).   ISBN 1-55337-739-7 (pbk.)

1. Refuse collectors — Juvenile literature. I. Bourgeois, Paulette. Canadian garbage
collectors. II. LaFave, Kim III. Title. III. Series: Kids Can read (Toronto, Ont.)

TD792.B68 2004   628.4'42'023   C2003-907468-4

Kids Can Press is a *l'©rus*™ Entertainment company

GARBAGE COLLECTORS

Paulette Bourgeois • Kim LaFave

Kids Can Press

A garbage truck rounds the corner.
It stops and starts. The brakes screech.
Sam, the garbage collector, runs back and
forth, back and forth. The garbage is heavy.
And there's lots of it.

"Hey, Sam," calls Mabel, the truck driver.
"I wonder where Mrs. Green is going in
such a hurry."

Sam wears a bright vest so that drivers can see him from far away.

Mabel squeezes the truck between parked cars. The children run towards it. Mabel shouts, "Please stay back!" She doesn't want them to get hurt by the truck.

"Is this a stinky job?" the children ask.

Sam laughs. "Only in the beginning. Now I'm used to it," he says. "But it can be messy. Sometimes the bags leak."

"Yuck," say the children. But Sam doesn't mind. He keeps clean clothes in the truck in case he has to change.

Sam tosses the bags into the hopper at
the back of the garbage truck.

All the garbage inside the truck can
weigh as much as an African elephant!

The truck keeps moving. It will stop at 500 houses today.

"Hey, Mabel, I think Mrs. Green has taken up jogging," Sam says.

There's hardly any garbage in front of Mark's house. That's because Mark's family follows the three R's: Reduce, Reuse and Recycle.

They use their bags and containers over and over again.

They use lunch boxes and Thermoses instead of bags and juice boxes.

They use cloth bags instead of paper or plastic.

They put newspapers, cans and clear glass in a recycling box.

They put leaves, vegetable peels, dead flowers, cut grass, egg shells, coffee grounds and tea bags into their composter.

A special truck picks up garbage that can be used again. Newspapers go in one bin. Clear glass goes in another bin. Cans go in another bin. Some plastic containers and some papers cannot be recycled.

Garbage that can be recycled goes to factories where it is made into other things. Glass can be ground up and used to make roads. Old newspaper is turned into cardboard or shingles for roofs. Cans are melted and made into new cans.

Some garbage is too dangerous for regular pick-up. This kind of garbage is called hazardous waste. It's taken to hazardous waste depots. Experts make sure it is buried or reused safely. Some cities have special trucks to pick up hazardous waste from homes.

Drain cleaners, oil paints, paint thinner, batteries and polish for metal and furniture are all hazardous waste. They should never be put out with regular garbage.

"Hey, Sam," says Mabel. "Mrs. Green keeps waving at you."

Whenever the hopper is full, Sam pulls the lever on the side of the truck. A wide metal blade moves down and crushes the garbage. Then the blade scoops the crushed garbage into the truck.

19

Just as Sam is about to pull the lever, Mrs. Green catches up. "Stop!" she cries. Mrs. Green whispers something to Sam.

Together they rip open the bags in the hopper. There, hidden between the chicken bones and the tea bags, are Mrs. Green's glasses.

When Mabel's truck is full, she drives
to the top level of a transfer station.
Mabel pushes a lever, and the garbage
empties out of her truck.
A bulldozer squishes
the garbage and shoves
it through a hole in
the floor into a huge
truck. This truck will
take the garbage to
a landfill site.

Most garbage is dumped into a hole in the ground at a landfill site. A bulldozer buries it. The garbage dump grows higher and higher until it becomes a garbage mountain.

In some places, garbage is burned. Some people think that burning garbage hurts plants and air and water.

In the country, people take their garbage to the dump themselves. Sometimes they find something they want to take home. As Mabel always says, "One person's garbage is somebody else's treasure."

At apartment buildings, the garbage is stored in large metal containers. A special garbage truck with arms picks up each container and empties it.

Some garbage
collectors collect trash
in the parks.

Others collect the litter off the
streets and sidewalks.

Even at night, garbage trucks move along quiet city streets. They pick up garbage from stores, office buildings and factories.

But garbage collectors don't always keep what they find. Just ask Sam and Mabel!